British
Lorries
of the 1950s

Those were the days ...™

VELOCE

Other great books from Veloce –

Speedpro Series
4-cylinder Engine – How To Blueprint & Build A Short Block For High Performance (Hammill)
Alfa Romeo DOHC High-performance Manual (Kartalamakis)
Alfa Romeo V6 Engine High-performance Manual (Kartalamakis)
BMC 998cc A-series Engine – How To Power Tune (Hammill)
1275cc A-series High-performance Manual (Hammill)
Camshafts – How To Choose & Time Them For Maximum Power (Hammill)
Competition Car Datalogging Manual, The (Templeman)
Cylinder Heads – How To Build, Modify & Power Tune Updated & Revised Edition (Burgess & Gollan)
Distributor-type Ignition Systems – How To Build & Power Tune New 3rd Edition (Hammill)
Fast Road Car – How To Plan And Build Revised & Updated Colour New Edition (Stapleton)
Ford SOHC 'Pinto' & Sierra Cosworth DOHC Engines – How To Power Tune Updated & Enlarged Edition (Hammill)
Ford V8 – How To Power Tune Small Block Engines (Hammill)
Harley-Davidson Evolution Engines – How To Build & Power Tune (Hammill)
Holley Carburetors – How To Build & Power Tune Revised & Updated Edition (Hammill)
Honda Civic Type R, High-Performance Manual ((Cowland & Clifford)
Jaguar XK Engines – How To Power Tune Revised & Updated Colour Edition (Hammill)
MG Midget & Austin-Healey Sprite – How To Power Tune New 3rd Edition (Stapleton)
MGB 4-cylinder Engine – How To Power Tune (Burgess)
MGB V8 Power – How To Give Your, Third Colour Edition (Williams)
MGB, MGC & MGB V8 – How To Improve New 2nd Edition (Williams)
Mini Engines – How To Power Tune On A Small Budget Colour Edition (Hammill)
Motorcycle-engined Racing Car – How To Build (Pashley)
Motorsport – Getting Started in (Collins)
Nissan GT-R High-performance Manual, The(Gorodji)
Nitrous Oxide High-performance Manual, The (Langfield)
Rover V8 Engines – How To Power Tune (Hammill)
Sportscar & Kitcar Suspension & Brakes – How To Build & Modify Revised 3rd Edition (Hammill)
SU Carburettor High-performance Manual (Hammill)
Successful Low-Cost Rally Car, How to Build a (Young)
Suzuki 4x4 – How To Modify For Serious Off-road Action (Richardson)
Tiger Avon Sportscar – How To Build Your Own Updated & Revised 2nd Edition (Dudley)
TR2, 3 & TR4 – How To Improve (Williams)
TR5, 250 & TR6 – How To Improve (Williams)
TR7 & TR8 – How To Improve (Williams)
V8 Engine – How To Build A Short Block For High Performance (Hammill)
Volkswagen Beetle Suspension, Brakes & Chassis – How To Modify For High Performance (Hale)
Volkswagen Bus Suspension, Brakes & Chassis – How To Modify For High Performance (Hale)
Weber DCOE, & Dellorto DHLA Carburetors – How To Build & Power Tune 3rd Edition (Hammill)

Those Were The Days ... Series
Alpine Trials & Rallies 1910-1973 (Pfundner)
American Trucks of the 1950s (Mort)
Anglo-American Cars From the 1930s to the 1970s (Mort)
Austerity Motoring (Bobbitt)
Austins, The last real (Peck)
Brighton National Speed Trials (Gardiner)
British Lorries Of The 1950s (Bobbitt)
British Lorries of the 1960s (Bonnitt)
British Touring Car Championship, The (Collins)
British Police Cars (Walker)
British Woodies (Peck)
Café Racer Phenomenon, The (Walker)
Dune Buggy Phenomenon (Hale)
Dune Buggy Phenomenon Volume 2 (Hale)
Hot Rod & Stock Car Racing in Britain In The 1980s (Neil)
Last Real Austins, The, 1946-1959 (Peck)
MG's Abingdon Factory (Moylan)
Motor Racing At Brands Hatch In The Seventies (Parker)
Motor Racing At Brands Hatch In The Eighties (Parker)
Motor Racing At Crystal Palace (Collins)
Motor Racing At Goodwood In The Sixties (Gardiner)
Motor Racing At Nassau In The 1950s & 1960s (O'Neil)
Motor Racing At Oulton Park In The 1960s (McFadyen)
Motor Racing At Oulton Park In The 1970s (McFadyen)
Superprix (Collins)
Three Wheelers (Bobbitt)

Enthusiast's Restoration Manual Series
Citroën 2CV, How To Restore (Porter)
Classic Car Bodywork, How To Restore (Thaddeus)
Classic British Car Electrical Systems (Astley)
Classic Car Electrics (Thaddeus)
Classic Cars, How To Paint (Thaddeus)
Reliant Regal, How To Restore (Payne)
Triumph TR2, 3, 3A, 4 & 4A, How To Restore (Williams)
Triumph TR5/250 & 6, How To Restore (Williams)
Triumph TR7/8, How To Restore (Williams)
Volkswagen Beetle, How To Restore (Tyler)
VW Bay Window Bus (Paxton)
Yamaha FS1-E, How To Restore (Watts)

Essential Buyer's Guide Series
Alfa GT (Booker)
Alfa Romeo Spider Giulia (Booker & Talbott)
BMW GS (Henshaw)
BSA Bantam (Henshaw)
BSA Twins (Henshaw)
Citroën 2CV (Paxton)
Citroën ID & DS (Heilig)
Fiat 500 & 600 (Bobbitt)
Ford Capri (Paxton)
Jaguar E-type 3.8 & 4.2-litre (Crespin)
Jaguar E-type V12 5.3-litre (Crespin)
Jaguar XJ 1995-2003 (Crespin)
Jaguar/Daimler XJ6, XJ12 & Sovereign (Crespin)
Jaguar/Daimler XJ40 (Crespin)
Jaguar XJ-S (Crespin)
MGB & MGB GT (Williams)
Mercedes-Benz 280SL-560DSL Roadsters (Bass)
Mercedes-Benz 'Pagoda' 230SL, 250SL & 280SL Roadsters & Coupés (Bass)
Mini (Paxton)
Morris Minor & 1000 (Newell)
Porsche 928 (Hemmings)
Rolls-Royce Silver Shadow & Bentley T-Series (Bobbitt)
Subaru Impreza (Hobbs)
Triumph Bonneville (Henshaw)
Triumph Stag (Mort & Fox)
Triumph TR6 (Williams)
VW Beetle (Cservenka & Copping)
VW Bus (Cservenka & Copping)
VW Golf GTI (Cservenka & Copping)

Auto-Graphics Series
Fiat-based Abarths (Sparrow)
Jaguar MKI & II Saloons (Sparrow)
Lambretta Li Series Scooters (Sparrow)

Rally Giants Series
Audi Quattro (Robson)
Austin Healey 100-6 & 3000 (Robson)
Fiat 131 Abarth (Robson)
Ford Escort MkI (Robson)
Ford Escort RS Cosworth & World Rally Car (Robson)
Ford Escort RS1800 (Robson)
Lancia Stratos (Robson)
Mini Cooper/Mini Cooper S (Robson)
Peugeot 205 T16 (Robson)
Subaru Impreza (Robson)
Toyota Celica GT4 (Robson)

WSC Giants
Ferrari 312P & 312PB (Collins & McDonough)

Battle Cry! Original Military Uniforms of the World
Soviet General & field rank officers uniforms: 1955 to 1991 (Streather)

General
1½-litre GP Racing 1961-1965 (Whitelock)
AC Two-litre Saloons & Buckland Sportscars (Archibald)
Alfa Romeo Giulia Coupé GT & GTA (Tipler)
Alfa Romeo Montreal – The dream car that came true (Taylor)
Alfa Romeo Montreal – The Essential Companion (Taylor)
Alfa Tipo 33 (McDonough & Collins)
Alpine & Renault – The Development Of The Revolutionary Turbo F1 Car 1968 to 1979 (Smith)
Anatomy Of The Works Minis (Moylan)
André Lefebvre, and the cars he created at Voisin and Citroën (Beck)
Armstrong-Siddeley (Smith)
Autodrome (Collins & Ireland)
Automotive A-Z, Lane's Dictionary Of Automotive Terms (Lane)
Automotive Mascots (Kay & Springate)
Bahamas Speed Weeks, The (O'Neil)
Bentley Continental, Corniche And Azure (Bennett)
Bentley MkVI, Rolls-Royce Silver Wraith, Dawn & Cloud/Bentley R & S-Series (Nutland)
BMC Competitions Department Secrets (Turner, Chambers Browning)
BMW 5-Series (Cranswick)
BMW Z-Cars (Taylor)
BMW Boxer Twins 1970-1995 Bible, The (Falloon)
Britains Farm Model Balers & Combines 1967-2007, Pocket Guide to (Pullen)
Britains Farm Model & Toy Tractors 1998-2008, Pocket Guide to (Pullen)
British 250cc Racing Motorcycles (Pereira)
British Cars, The Complete Catalogue Of, 1895-1975 (Culshaw & Horrobin)
BRM – A Mechanic's Tale (Salmon)
BRM V16 (Ludvigsen)
BSA Bantam Bible, The (Henshaw)
Bugatti Type 40 (Price)
Bugatti 46/50 Updated Edition (Price & Arbey)
Bugatti T44 & T49 (Price & Arbey)
Bugatti 57 2nd Edition (Price)
Caravans, The Illustrated History 1919-1959 (Jenkinson)
Caravans, The Illustrated History From 1960 (Jenkinson)
Carrera Panamericana, La (Tipler)
Chrysler 300 – America's Most Powerful Car 2nd Edition (Ackerson)
Chrysler PT Cruiser (Ackerson)
Citroën DS (Bobbitt)
Classic British Car Electrical Systems (Astley)
Cliff Allison – From The Fells To Ferrari (Gauld)
Cobra – The Real Thing! (Legate)
Concept Cars, How to illustrate and design (Dewey)
Cortina – Ford's Bestseller (Robson)
Coventry Climax Racing Engines (Hammill)
Daimler SP250 New Edition (Long)
Datsun Fairlady Roadster To 280ZX – The Z-Car Story (Long)
Diecast Toy Cars of the 1950s & 1960s (Ralston)
Dino – The V6 Ferrari (Long)
Dodge Challenger & Plymouth Barracuda (Grist)
Dodge Charger – Enduring Thunder (Ackerson)
Dodge Dynamite! (Grist)
Donington (Boddy)
Draw & Paint Cars – How To (Gardiner)
Drive On The Wild Side, A – 20 Extreme Driving Adventures From Around The World (Weaver)
Ducati 750 Bible, The (Falloon)
Ducati 860, 900 And Mille Bible, The (Falloon)
Dune Buggy, Building A – The Essential Manual (Shakespeare)
Dune Buggy Files (Hale)
Dune Buggy Handbook (Hale)
Edward Turner: The Man Behind The Motorcycles (Clew)
Fast Ladies – Female Racing Drivers 1888 to 1970 (Bouzanquet)
Fiat & Abarth 124 Spider & Coupé (Tipler)
Fiat & Abarth 500 & 600 2nd Edition (Bobbitt)
Fiats, Great Small (Ward)
Fine Art Of The Motorcycle Engine, The (Peirce)
Ford F100/F150 Pick-up 1948-1996 (Ackerson)
Ford F150 Pick-up 1997-2005 (Ackerson)
Ford GT – Then, And Now (Streather)
Ford GT40 (Legate)
Ford In Miniature (Olson)
Ford Model Y (Roberts)
Ford Thunderbird From 1954, The Book Of The (Long)
Formula 5000 Motor Racing, Back then ... and back now (Lawson)
Forza Minardi! (Vigar)
Funky Mopeds (Skelton)
Gentleman Jack (Gauld)
GM In Miniature (Olson)
GT – The World's Best GT Cars 1953-73 (Dawson)
Hillclimbing & Sprinting – The Essential Manual (Short & Wilkinson)
Honda NSX (Long)
Intermeccanica - The Story of the Prancing Bull (McCredie & Reisner)
Jaguar, The Rise Of (Price)
Jaguar XJ-S (Long)
Jeep CJ (Ackerson)
Jeep Wrangler (Ackerson)
John Chatham – 'Mr Big Healey' – The Official Biography (Burr)
Karmann-Ghia Coupé & Convertible (Bobbitt)
Lamborghini Miura Bible, The (Sackey)
Lambretta Bible, The (Davies)
Lancia 037 (Collins)
Lancia Delta HF Integrale (Blaettel & Wagner)
Land Rover, The Half-ton Military (Cook)
Laverda Twins & Triples Bible 1968-1986 (Falloon)
Lea-Francis Story, The (Price)
Lexus Story, The (Long)
little book of smart, the New Edition (Jackson)
Lola – The Illustrated History (1957-1977) (Starkey)
Lola – All The Sports Racing & Single-seater Racing Cars 1978-1997 (Starkey)
Lola T70 – The Racing History & Individual Chassis Record 4th Edition (Starkey)
Lotus 49 (Oliver)
Marketingmobiles, The Wonderful Wacky World Of (Hale)
Mazda MX-5/Miata 1.6 Enthusiast's Workshop Manual (Grainger & Shoemark)
Mazda MX-5/Miata 1.8 Enthusiast's Workshop Manual (Grainger & Shoemark)
Mazda MX-5 Miata: The Book Of The World's Favourite Sportscar (Long)
Mazda MX-5 Miata Roadster (Long)
Maximum Mini (Booij)
MGA (Price Williams)
MGB & MGB GT– Expert Guide (Auto-doc Series) (Williams)
MGB Electrical Systems Updated & Revised Edition (Astley)
Micro Caravans (Jenkinson)
Micro Trucks (Mort)
Microcars At Large! (Quellin)
Mini Cooper – The Real Thing! (Tipler)
Mitsubishi Lancer Evo, The Road Car & WRC Story (Long)
Montlhéry, The Story Of The Paris Autodrome (Boddy)
Morgan Maverick (Lawrence)
Morris Minor, 60 Years On The Road (Newell)
Moto Guzzi Sport & Le Mans Bible, The (Falloon)
Motor Movies – The Posters! (Veysey)
Motor Racing – Reflections Of A Lost Era (Carter)
Motorcycle Apprentice (Cakebread)
Motorcycle Road & Racing Chassis Designs (Noakes)
Motorhomes, The Illustrated History (Jenkinson)
Motorsport In colour, 1950s (Wainwright)
Nissan 300ZX & 350Z – The Z-Car Story (Long)
Nissan GT-R Supercar: Born to race (Gorodji)
Off-Road Giants! – Heroes of 1960s Motorcycle Sport (Westlake)
Pass The Theory And Practical Driving Tests (Gibson & Hoole)
Peking To Paris 2007 (Young)
Plastic Toy Cars Of The 1950s & 1960s (Ralston)
Pontiac Firebird (Cranswick)
Porsche Boxster (Long)
Porsche 356 (2nd Edition) (Long)
Porsche 908 (Födisch, Neßhöver, Roßbach, Schwarz & Roßbach)
Porsche 911 Carrera – The Last Of The Evolution (Corlett)
Porsche 911R, RS & RSR, 4th Edition (Starkey)
Porsche 911 – The Definitive History 1963-1971 (Long)
Porsche 911 – The Definitive History 1971-1977 (Long)
Porsche 911 – The Definitive History 1977-1987 (Long)
Porsche 911 – The Definitive History 1987-1997 (Long)
Porsche 911 – The Definitive History 1997-2004 (Long)
Porsche 911SC 'Super Carrera' – The Essential Companion (Streather)
Porsche 914 & 914-6: The Definitive History Of The Road & Competition Cars (Long)
Porsche 924 (Long)
Porsche 928 (Long)
Porsche 944 (Long)
Porsche 964, 993 & 996 Data Plate Code Breaker (Streather)
Porsche 993 'King Of Porsche' – The Essential Companion (Streather)
Porsche 996 'Supreme Porsche' – The Essential Companion (Streather)
Porsche Racing Cars – 1953 To 1975 (Long)
Porsche Racing Cars – 1976 To 2005 (Long)
Porsche – The Rally Story (Meredith)
Porsche: Three Generations Of Genius (Meredith)
RAC Rally Action! (Gardiner)
Rallye Sport Fords: The Inside Story (Moreton)
Redman, Jim – 6 Times World Motorcycle Champion: The Autobiography (Redman)
Rolls-Royce Silver Shadow/Bentley T Series Corniche & Camargue Revised & Enlarged Edition (Bobbitt)
Rolls-Royce Silver Spirit, Silver Spur & Bentley Mulsanne 2nd Edition (Bobbitt)
Russian Motor Vehicles (Kelly)
RX-7 – Mazda's Rotary Engine Sportscar (Updated & Revised New Edition) (Long)
Save the Triumph Bonneville! – The inside story of the Meriden workers' co-op (Rosamond)
Scooters & Microcars, The A-Z Of Popular (Dan)
Scooter Lifestyle (Grainger)
Singer Story: Cars, Commercial Vehicles, Bicycles & Motorcycle (Atkinson)
SM – Citroën's Maserati-engined Supercar (Long & Claverol)
Speedway – Auto Racing's Ghost Tracks (Collins & Ireland)
Subaru Impreza: The Road Car And WRC Story (Long)
Supercar, How To Build your own (Thompson)
Tales from the Toolbox (Oliver)
Taxi! The Story Of The 'London' Taxicab (Bobbitt)
Tinplate Toy Cars Of The 1950s & 1960s (Ralston)
Toleman Story, The (Hilton)
Toyota Celica & Supra, The Book Of Toyota's Sports Coupés (Long)
Toyota MR2 Coupés & Spyders (Long)
Triumph Motorcycles & The Meriden Factory (Hancox)
Triumph Motorcycles - The Meriden Workers' Co-op Chronicles (Rosamund)
Triumph Speed Twin & Thunderbird Bible (Woolridge)
Triumph Tiger Cub Bible (Estall)
Triumph Trophy Bible (Woolridge)
Triumph TR6 (Kimberley)
Unraced (Collins)
Velocette Motorcycles – MSS To Thruxton Updated & Revised (Burris)
Virgil Exner – Visioneer: The Official Biography Of Virgil M Exner Designer Extraordinaire (Grist)
Volkswagen Bus Book, The (Bobbitt)
Volkswagen Bus Or Van To Camper, How To Convert (Porter)
Volkswagens Of The World (Glen)
VW Beetle Cabriolet (Bobbitt)
VW Beetle – The Car Of The 20th Century (Copping)
VW Bus – 40 Years Of Splitties, Bays & Wedges (Copping)
VW Bus Book, The (Bobbitt)
VW Golf: Five Generations Of Fun (Copping & Cservenka)
VW – The Air-cooled Era (Copping)
VW T5 Camper Conversion Manual (Porter)
VW Campers (Copping)
Works Minis, The Last (Purves & Brenchley)
Works Rally Mechanic (Moylan)

www.veloce.co.uk

First published in April 2009 by Veloce Publishing Limited, 33 Trinity Street, Dorchester DT1 1TT, England. Fax 01305 268864/e-mail info@veloce.co.uk/web www.veloce.co.uk or www.velocebooks.com.
ISBN: 978-1-84584-209-3/UPC: 6-36847-04209-7

Readers with ideas for automotive books, or books on other transport or related hobby subjects, are invited to write to the editorial director of Veloce Publishing at the above address.
British Library Cataloguing in Publication Data - A catalogue record for this book is available from the British Library. Typesetting, design and page make-up all by Veloce Publishing Ltd on Apple Mac. Printed in India by Replika Press.

Contents

Introduction and acknowledgements

The lorry, 'King of the Road', is an intrinsic part of Britain's road scene. Carriers of everything in the nation's shopping baskets, lorries large and small have, since the very beginnings of the motor transport industry, performed tasks of immeasurable value. A familiar sight on minor roads as well as motorways, today it is easy to overlook the importance these vehicles play when it comes to the country's economy. Without these leviathans, supermarket shelves would be empty, garages without fuel, and our homes would lack the everyday items we take for granted.

In the 1950s, motorways had yet to make their mark on Britain's landscape. Changes were afoot, however. Lorry manufacturers were introducing new designs of vehicles to make use of advancing technology, and the building of bypasses around some of the larger and most congested towns meant that vehicles could travel further and faster than ever before. The autoroute, already familiar on mainland Europe, was destined for the United Kingdom. By the end of the decade lorry drivers had a glimpse of the future when they travelled along the newly opened Preston bypass, the beginning of Britain's motorway network.

The pages that follow contain some evocative names: AEC, Albion, Bedford, Commer, ERF, Leyland, Foden, Maudslay, Scammell, Thames and Thornycroft to name but a few. Whilst these and other vehicles kept Britain moving, it is essential to remember that not a wheel would have turned had it not been for the people who designed and built them, and not least the drivers who steered their charges up and down the country, night and day, summer and winter.

Venturing into the world of British lorries of the 1950s has been an enjoyable experience, except that a lorry, whatever its age, will never quite seem the same again! I am grateful to the many people who have helped me compile this book. John Burrow introduced me to various vehicle owners and John Curwen allowed me to trawl through his extensive photographic collection.

My thanks are extended to the kind folk who let me photograph their vehicles. Gratitude is expressed to motoring researcher and historian Andrew Minney for his helpful comments and guidance in respect of some of the more obscure areas of the British commercial vehicle industry. Not least, my thanks go to my wife Jean who has had to endure my rushing off to photograph lorries, and who continues to worry about my sanity.

Every effort has been made to trace the copyright of photographs and illustrations. If as a result any copyright has not been acknowledged, I offer my sincere apologies.

Malcolm Bobbitt
Cockermouth, Cumbria

This London scene typically represents the early 1950s. The location is Covent Garden, the lorry in the foreground being a prewar Leyland. Parked behind it is a Scammell three-wheeler Scarab tractor unit wearing British Railways livery. Two Bedfords can be seen; one is parked outside the Kings Arms public house and is operated by TS Barnard, the other, in the background, is owned by Grove Motors. There is no indication as to the date, though the type of Bedfords dicate it be post-1953. The fact that the street cleaner seen behind the Scarab is wearing shirt sleeves suggests it is a spring or summer day.
(John Curwen collection/Hub Publishing)

Postwar austerity

The immediate postwar years were difficult times for the road haulage industry. It was effectively being run with prewar vehicles, and hauliers had to wait until the early 1950s before new designs of lorries emerged onto the market.

Morris Commercial C8s were commonly seen on Britain's roads during the years of austerity. This now well-used example was supplied new to the Ministry of Defence in 1940 and demobbed in 1947; thereafter it was used for farm work before being converted to a breakdown truck in 1956. (Author's collection)

In addition to being used on public service, the AEC Matador found favour with the British Army in WW2. After hostilities ceased, many Matadors were pressed into service by haulage companies, and became a familiar sight in the early 1950s, like this 1939 example wearing Salford transport decals. (Author's collection)

The growth in road freight transport was phenomenal. When goods licensing was introduced in 1933 there were around 450,000 commercial vehicles in use, the figure increasing to 480,000 by 1937, and to 670,000 in 1947. Thereafter, with manufacturers getting production fully under way, the surge in the number of private goods haulage (C-licensed) vehicles meant that nearly half a million were registered between 1946 and 1952.

With the prospect of nationalisation and the establishment of the British Transport Commission, the late 1940s and early 50s was a period of uncertainty. Though the Transport Bill passed into law in August 1947, it was so watered down that only part of the long-distance road transport industry was nationalised, all C-licensed haulage remaining in private hands.

An ex-military AEC Matador of 1944 vintage makes its way through the Westmorland town of Kirkby Stephen, situated high up in the north Pennines. Such all-wheel drive vehicles, which were officially gun tractors, found useful employment in desert conditions and for extricating other vehicles from soft terrain. (Author's collection)

Austins were a common sight at the turn of the decade, this example wearing a registration first issued in April 1949. Owned by Holbrooke Motors of Otley in Yorkshire and looking resplendent, it is seen in company with an early postwar Scammell. (Author's collection)

Pictured in the early 1950s, this 1948 Austin tanker in service with JHBL Oil Products leads an Austin coach along a seaside promenade. Parked on the jetty in the background can be seen a variety of 1950s cars, including a Vauxhall, Morris Eight, and a couple of split-screen Morris Minors. (John Curwen collection/Hub Publishing)

Of similar vintage to the Austins in the previous pictures is this 1949 Morris Commercial. Vehicles of this type were used for many years after the war, a number of them utilised by British Railways. The Morris in this instance is painted GWR brown and cream. (Author's collection)

Behind the December 1952-registered North Thames Gas Atkinson, pictured near Euston, is one of the 250,000 Bedford War Department vehicles that were built in Britain's 'shadow' factories. Many were transferred to the private sector after wartime where they continued to give sterling service. (John Curwen collection/Hub Publishing)

A number of Bedford WD vehicles have been preserved; 9847 AH wears the livery of A&D Golightly, haulage contractor of Hunwick in County Durham. Cumberland-registered 397 GRM has a hatch above the passenger seat, indicating that the vehicle was built for military purposes. Note the cable-operated semaphore on the nearside; when turning right, the driver would be expected to make a hand signal. In peacetime these 15cwt lorries were often used as breakdown trucks. (Author's collection)

The tractor unit leading the fleet of factory-fresh postwar Bedford pick-ups has delivery labels affixed to the windscreen. Bedford's range of lorries comprised payloads from 5/6cwt to 5 tons. (John Curwen collection)

The familiar profile of the immediate postwar Bedford. In addition to lorries, these Bedfords, which were built from 1945 until 1953, formed the basis of many bus and coach fleets. The 1952 Bedford OB pictured has been carefully restored, its 28hp petrol engine returning 13-14mpg. (Author's collection)

The prewar Leyland Hippo in service with British Road Services' Parcels Service, post-1951. Photographed outside a brewery, the car parked behind the lorry is a Ford Pilot carrying a 1951 London registration. Pilots were expensive cars, and this example might have belonged to one of the brewery directors. (John Curwen collection/Hub Publishing)

Lorry builder Thornycroft celebrated its Golden Jubilee in 1946, the breakdown truck seen here having originated from around that time. The vehicle was photographed when in service at Thornycroft's Manchester service branch. Thornycroft also operated service depots in Birmingham, Cardiff, Glasgow, Leeds, London and Newcastle. (Author's collection)

In addition to its service branches, Thornycroft operated an apprentice training school at West Ham House in Surrey. Detached from the works, the workshop afforded full hands-on training, these apprentices being under instruction. Boys could join the company at the age of 14, and at 16 begin a 5-year apprenticeship. (Author's collection)

Prewar, Sentinel was closely associated with steam vehicles, the last examples being built in 1950. The first Sentinel petrol lorry appeared in 1945, and a year later a diesel, as pictured, appeared. Four-wheeled Sentinels were built with a variety of bodies, including pick-ups and tippers. (Author's collection)

Since the 1930s AEC had a tradition of naming its models beginning with the letter M, hence Matador and, as seen here, Mammoth Major. In service with coal merchant Howdens of Larne in Northern Ireland, this 1947 vehicle appears to be in new condition. (John Curwen collection)

Scammell lorries are synonymous with heavy haulage, the firm having been established at Watford in Hertfordshire since 1922. Vehicles such as the example seen here in service with Jarvis Robinson Transport Ltd of Liverpool were a familiar sight on Britain's roads in the 1930s and postwar. Depicted in service with Whitbread, this type of postwar rigid eight-wheeler was the basis of many a haulage company, the standard machines having single axle drive, with the double axle drive reserved for more arduous uses. (John Curwen collection/Blunden; author's collection)

Another famous name lorry manufacturer is Foden, this 1949/50 vehicle pictured in service with sand merchant Joseph Adshead of Ringway, Manchester. Foden, once renowned for its steam engines, switched to diesel power in the 1930s to rival ERF, which was established by ER Foden as a separate enterprise. (Author's collection)

Another AEC Mammoth, pictured here in operation with British Road Services, the firm established as part of the Labour government's nationalisation scheme. This 8-wheeler carries a Norfolk registration dating from 1949.
(John Curwen collection/Hub Publishing)

Lorries like this 1950 Guy Otter helped keep Britain on the move during the period of austerity. This preserved example in Silentnight apparel was photographed in 2007 at the Kirkby Stephen and Brough Vintage Commercial weekend, held annually in the north Pennines over the Easter weekend. (Author's collection)

This busy scene depicts an Albion lorry in service with Rowe Bros of Bristol, being loaded in early postwar days. The fact that the lorry isn't wearing a registration plate suggests that the photograph was contrived for publicity purposes. (John Curwen collection)

The Dennis Pax brochure of 1947 shows a vehicle delivering beer to a country pub. Here, a similar vehicle is seen outside the Marquis of Westminster in London's Belgrave Road in early postwar days, with a delivery of Watney's Ale. The absence of traffic suggests the delivery was made early morning. (John Curwen collection/Truc-Foto)

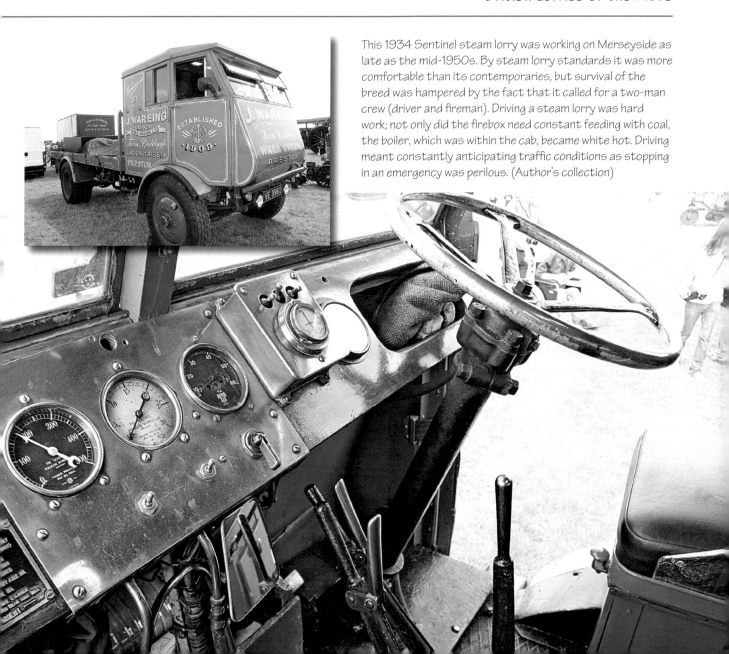

This 1934 Sentinel steam lorry was working on Merseyside as late as the mid-1950s. By steam lorry standards it was more comfortable than its contemporaries, but survival of the breed was hampered by the fact that it called for a two-man crew (driver and fireman). Driving a steam lorry was hard work; not only did the firebox need constant feeding with coal, the boiler, which was within the cab, became white hot. Driving meant constantly anticipating traffic conditions as stopping in an emergency was perilous. (Author's collection)

Seen leaving their Guildford Street, SE1 London depot early postwar, these two prewar AECs are Swansea-bound. The driver of the leading Andrews vehicle appears to be in discussion with either the transport or despatch manager, but, in any event, both lorries are in sparkling condition. (John Curwen collection/Truc-Foto)

Delivering on time

At the beginning of the 1950s much work was necessary to rebuild the fabric of British society, torn to shreds by the war. Not least was the need to get industry, commerce and transport moving at full speed.

Unlike mainland Europe, where ambitious road building programmes were under way, Britain's road system remained much the same as it was prewar. It was not until the end of the decade, when the Preston bypass opened, that motorway travel became a reality.

Getting Britain on the move meant transporting building materials for factories and new towns. Foodstuffs had to be carried from producer to retailer, and raw materials were needed for manufacturing purposes. Once the wheels of industry were turning,

keeping Britain on the move was essential. Maintaining fuel supplies was crucial, and whether a one-man business or a fleet operation, keeping vehicles running day and night throughout the year called not only for drivers, but also qualified motor engineers.

Mechanical Horses were an intrinsic part of the local delivery scene. This 1946-registered Scammell 3-ton vehicle is pictured in London in the early 1950s delivering crates of Watney's Pale Ale to a London public house. Note that the tractor unit has the steering wheel centrally located in line with the single front wheel.
(John Curwen collection/Truc-Foto)

A frequent sight at docks and railway stations around the country was the Scammell Scarab Beetle, depicted in this publicity image. In use, this model was more practical than the type it replaced, the position of the engine, at the rear of the cab, allowing greater stability when manoeuvring in tight spaces. (Author's collection)

Local delivery services were the domain of light commercials, the like of this Thames 2-ton van photographed on a wet day in the early 1950s. These vehicles had V8 30hp petrol engines, wide opening doors at the rear giving access to a 450ft^3 load area, and sliding doors to the driver's compartment. (Author's collection)

This 1957 Seddon Twenty Five is a rare survivor. It served for some time as Seddon Vehicles' service van, and was fitted with a Perkins P3-144 2660cc diesel engine. Restoration has been a lengthy business, and the vehicle is pictured here in 2008 in the north of England. (Author's collection)

With the establishment of the British Motor Corporation in 1952, both Austin and Morris were contenders in the lighter payload market. Pictured is the Morris version of the forward-control 5-ton pick-up, which was initially specified with a 6-cylinder 4.5-litre petrol engine. The diesel engine vehicle was fitted with an 'economy overdrive' gearbox as standard. (Author's collection)

Delivering on time

This 1955-registered, preserved Austin 303 was originally owned by Citroën Cars Ltd of Slough in Buckinghamshire as a works vehicle. One of its prime uses was to collect glass fibre bodyshells from coachbuilder James Whitson in connection with the Bijou, which was a British-built version of the ubiquitous Citroën 2CV. The lorry was sold to Vandervell Bros Ltd in 1959. (Courtesy Michael Parker)

This Wells (Somerset) based British Road Services Austin 303 3-ton lorry wears a 1956 registration and is successor to the Austin version of the Morris shown on the previous page. The Austin depicted here is identical to its Morris-badged sibling, except for minor differences to the front grille. (John Curwen collection)

RIGHT UP YOUR STREET!

Carrying your burdens swiftly, easily and economically, the new Morris 2-tonner is the smart, reliable job you've been looking for to increase the range of your business. This truck is versatile enough to carry all sorts of goods and sturdy enough to support a generous load on its twin rear wheels. Economically run on diesel fuel*, it is fast, clean-lined and easily manœuvrable. Ask your Morris dealer for more details.

*Available also with 4-cylinder petrol engine

WITH TWELVE MONTHS' WARRANTY

THE NEW **MORRIS**

LIGHT TWO-TON TRUCK

MC 7/40

MORRIS COMMERCIAL CARS LTD., ADDERLEY PARK, BIRMINGHAM, Overseas Business: Nuffield Exports Ltd., Oxford and 41, Piccadilly, London, W

B23

By the time this publicity item for the Morris LC 2-tonner appeared in November 1956, the model was at the end of its life. The advertisement does, nevertheless, impart a sense of urgency in the rush to build on Britain's growing prosperity in the mid-1950s.

This is typical of the period artwork featured in this book, with the emphasis on the vehicle's 'muscle power,' the friendly attitude of the driver (who is not always in proportion to the vehicle or scene), and the uniformed inspector. Note the advertisement blurb, which says that the Morris Two-Ton Truck is available with a petrol engine, suggesting opposition by some customers to diesel power.
(Author's collection)

Known as the Loadstar until the formation of BMC, Austin's 5-ton lorry was available in a number of configurations. Contemporary publicity material depicts the lorry as being dependable in the rapid carriage of perishable goods. The Austin seen here was pictured before entering service with Mutual Meat Traders Ltd of Bristol. (John Curwen collection)

THE COMMERCIAL MOTOR, APRIL 30, 1954 COLOUR 17

NUMBER
15
SHED

Toughest Truck in the Business !

HERE'S the Austin 5-tonner, the toughest, longest-lasting truck in the transport business.

A big claim? This is a big truck. Big enough to move five tons of whatever you want moving. Big-hearted enough to work whenever and wherever you want work done, year in, year out and round the clock if need be. And smart enough to carry any firm's name.

What else do you want? Dependability? A Midlands firm writes saying their Austin has "run 105,000 miles and required no major replacements for engine, chassis or body during that time". Economy? A *Commercial Motor* road test proved the Austin to be "among the most economical of its class". And added, "The Austin lorry has better dust-proofing to the cab than many British cars".

This Austin has everything you want from a truck.

FREE BOOK. A price list and full information about the Austin truck range gladly sent on request. Write on your business notepaper to: The Sales Department, The Austin Motor Company Limited, Longbridge, Birmingham.

AUSTIN — you can depend on it !

THE AUSTIN MOTOR COMPANY LIMITED • LONGBRIDGE • BIRMINGHAM

Under the auspices of BMC, Austin was promoted by some bold publicity material proclaiming the marque to be the "Toughest Truck in the Business!" The artwork exemplifies the need to keep business on the move, and not least the importance of Britain's import and export trading. (Author's collection)

Though part of the Chrysler Corporation of America, Dodge Trucks were assembled in Britain at Kew and, therefore, were considered to be British. To a great extent Dodge was overshadowed by its rival, General Motors-owned Bedford. The Dodge seen here is in service with the Airscrew Co Ltd and Jigwood Ltd of Weybridge in Surrey. (John Curwen collection/Truc-Foto)

Leyland bought Scottish lorry maker Albion in 1951 and, in the mid-1950s, introduced a model with an underfloor diesel engine. The Claymore, a late 1950s example seen here in Golden Shred Marmalade livery, was available as a 4 or 5-tonner with the option of a 5 or 6-speed gearbox. (John Curwen collection)

A rather more familiar face for Albions of the 1950s is the Chieftain, the firm's first dedicated lorry in postwar years. It was specified with Albion's own 4.88-litre diesel engine, which produced 76bhp at 2000rpm.
(Author's collection)

The Maudslay is often mistaken for an AEC, owing to the style of radiator and badge. Established in 1901, the Maudslay Motor Company was acquired by Associated Commercial Vehicles in 1948, and, within three years, Maudslays became, in effect, rebadged AECs. The lorry seen here is a Meritor. (John Curwen collection)

(Below) A Graesser Chemicals (Chester) AEC Mandator makes its way through north London around 1954/5. The vehicle, followed by a Ford Anglia, would have had either a 9.6 or 11.3-litre diesel engine coupled to a five or six-speed gearbox, and is seen overtaking a line of trolleybuses, which in all probability would have been AEC-built.
(John Curwen collection/Hub Publishing)

Power and speed is the message in this evocative piece of mid-1950s advertising material. The AEC Mammoth Major as depicted is, in this instance, sharing publicity in association with clutch and transmission specialist Borg & Beck.
(Author's collection)

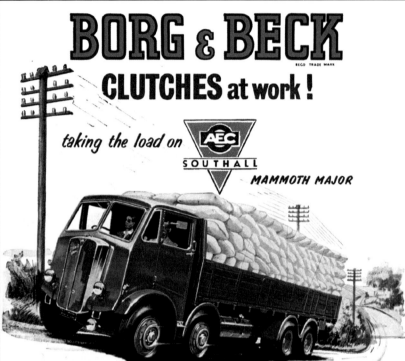

BORG & BECK

REGD TRADE MARK

CLUTCHES at work !

taking the load on **AEC** SOUTHALL

MAMMOTH MAJOR

COMPLETE RANGE OF HEAVY DUTY FRICTION PLATES FOR EVERY COMMERCIAL VEHICLE

And the loads taken by these heavy duty vehicles need some pulling up and down the hills on present day roads. The power provided by the A.E.C. diesel engine is transmitted for four wheel drive by the Borg & Beck heavy duty clutch—smoothly and never failing, so important when gears are used for braking such heavy loads.

A.E.C. know that they can rely on clutches by the specialists, as also do the manufacturers of 82% of British vehicles.

FOR CLUTCH RELIABILITY *BE SURE AND CHECK IT'S A BORG & BECK*

BORG & BECK COMPANY LTD., LEAMINGTON SPA, WARWICKSHIRE

Photographed outside Rover distributor Charles Hurst Ltd, this dust-covered Londonderry-registered AEC eight-wheeler belonged to the Northern Sand & Brick Co of Belfast. (John Curwen collection)

This London County Council Leyland Beaver is stablemate to the AECs seen previously. At the back of the low-loader trailer unit is a forklift truck, ready, no doubt, to lift the cargo of concrete blocks. Might the lorry crew be inside the Mayfair Café? (John Curwen collection/Hub Publishing)

THE COMMERCIAL MOTOR

FRIDAY, SEPTEMBER 28, 1956
NINEPENCE

SHOW TECHNICAL REVIEW

LCO 1956

Leyland 7-8 ton COMET
THE FAMOUS ECONOMY TRUCK

So far... for so little... for so long!

LEYLAND MOTORS LTD. LEYLAND · LANCS · ENGLAND Sales Division: HANOVER HOUSE, HANOVER SQUARE, LONDON W.1.

(Above) Announced in 1947 and remaining in production until the mid-1950s, the 5-7-ton Comet was Leyland's first all-new postwar truck. Comets were available in three configurations: Haulage, Tipper and Tractor; a preserved example of the first is seen here, owned by Peter and Joyce Thompson. (Joyce Thompson)

This evocative piece of artwork graced the cover of the 1956 *Commercial Motor* Show edition of *The Commercial Motor*. Depicted is the 7-8-ton Leyland Comet, which replaced the vehicle seen in the above photograph. It says everything about the workhorse it proved to be. (Author's collection)

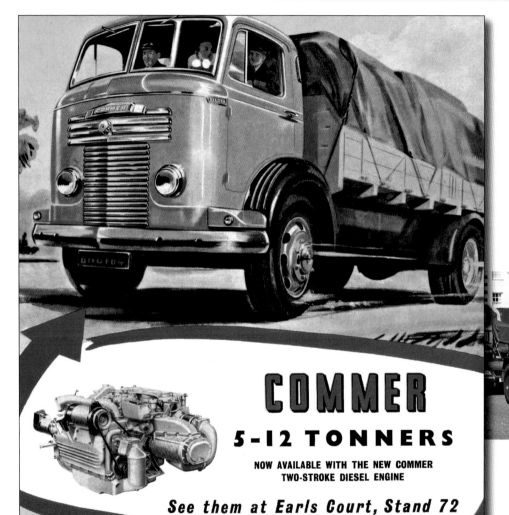

Commer began life as
Commercial Cars in 1905,
and was bought by Humber
in 1926, when the Commer
name came into being. In 1928
Humber and Commer were
absorbed into the Rootes
empire, but it was not until
the early postwar years
that an underfloor-engined
lorry, as depicted here, was
introduced.
(Author's collection)

COMMER

5-12 TONNERS

**NOW AVAILABLE WITH THE NEW COMMER
TWO-STROKE DIESEL ENGINE**

See them at Earls Court, Stand 72

PRODUCTS OF THE ROOTES GROUP

Commer underfloor-engined
lorries were popular with
hauliers, the optional 2-stroke
diesel engine having been
developed by Tilling Stevens
before being acquired by
Rootes in 1951.
(Author's collection)

Sentinel

AI service on the AI and throughout Britain

Map flags:
- MITCHELLS GARAGE (STONEHAVEN) LTD
- W. D. WATT & CO BROUGHTYFERRY
- EDINBURGH MOTOR ENGINEERING CO LTD
- K & B MOTORS NEWCASTLE-ON-TYNE
- WILKS & MEADE LTD LEEDS
- THOMAS HILL (ROTHERHAM) LTD
- RUFFORD MOTOR CO LTD MANSFIELD
- WIGGS & SONS LTD LONDON SE 15
- JAMES WHITSON & SONS LTD WEST DRAYTON

Sentinel of Shrewsbury enjoyed an enviable reputation, but in postwar years it had difficulty competing against rival manufacturers. The publicity material illustrated must have been one of the company's last advertising projects before the remnants of Sentinel's stock were sold to Transport Vehicles Ltd of Cheshire. (Author's collection)

Thornycroft is another lorry maker associated with steam vehicles. This Nippy was delivered to Messrs Style & Winch in 1955, when first registered. By 1955 standards the lorry cab, which was designed in 1943, appears distinctly dated.
(John Curwen collection/Truc-Foto)

The interior of the Motor Panels GRP cab as fitted to an early 1950s Thornycroft. Though it appears spartan by today's standard, it nevertheless afforded the height of luxury. The leather upholstered seats had little adjustment and the instrumentation was minimal, but at least the quilted engine cover hatch deadened some of the noise. (Author's collection)

FLOWERS

FLOWERS SABLE STOUT

LIQUID LUXURY

CBR 664

61

61

Streamlined and much more modern-looking than the vehicle in the previous photograph, this lorry has a Motor Panels cab. The vehicle's registration number dates from 1952, around the time when glass-reinforced resin cabs were being fitted to Thornycroft's Trident and Nippy models. (John Curwen collection/Truc-Foto)

The name of Atkinson is inextricably linked with Sentinel, the former having originally been a sales outlet for the latter. Atkinson came into its own after 1933 and was a major player during WW2, after which, in 1952, Atkinson Lorries changed its name to Atkinson Vehicles Ltd. During the early postwar years Atkinson kept its prewar image; this heavily laden lorry is pictured in the late 1950s. (John Curwen collection/Hub Publishing)

A later Atkinson than that seen in the previous photograph is pictured here wearing British Road Services livery, though the date (it has to be later than 1954) and location are unrecorded. Note the starting handle protruding from the lorry's radiator grille; only a brave person would contemplate swinging it! (John Curwen collection/Hub Publishing)

See why **Foden** LEADS 1856 1956

ON STAND 59
COMMERCIAL MOTOR SHOW, SEPT. 21st to 29th.

You've got to be good to be in business 100 years

FODENS LIMITED · SANDBACH · CHESHIRE

Foden is a leading name in lorries, and celebrated its centenary in 1956. As has been mentioned elsewhere, there is a family link between ERF and Foden, the latter's factory being situated at Sandbach in Cheshire. Visibility from the type of cab introduced in the mid-1950s was good, despite its dated appearance. (Author's collection)

Peter and Joyce Thompson's Foden S20 lorry pictured during its working life when in service with Breedon and Cloud Hill Quarry of Derby during the mid-1950s. Fodens were unwavering workhorses, which is one reason why so many have survived the passage of time. (Peter & Joyce Thompson)

The Foden S20 now restored to its present gleaming condition. The Foden eight-wheeler is powered by a Gardiner 150 diesel engine and could manage a payload of 24 tons. (Peter & Joyce Thompson)

Were coal deliveries really like this in the early 1950s? Coal lorries were usually covered with black dust and the delivery men wore leather jackets complete with caps that draped to form shoulder protection. Ford 4 and 5-tonners were fitted with Ford's own 3622cc V8 petrol engine, though it was possible to specify the Perkins P-6 4732cc diesel. Holder of the Royal Warrant, Franklin's Coals, it would appear, was a fuel merchant of high repute. (Ford/author's collection)

Delivering on time

A wide range of vehicles comprised the Ford range for the early 1950s. The Thames truck could be specified in a number of guises, from 2-ton vans, 2, 3, 4 and 5-ton pick-ups, 4 cubic yard tippers and the Sussex 6-wheeler chassis and cab. There were refuse loaders, cesspool emptiers and tractor units, as well as special purpose vehicles, some of which were for export only. Selling points for the vehicles included easy engine accessibility, v-shaped windscreen (said to aid visibility in brilliant sun or at night), and an electric windscreen wiper to ensure clear vision in the rain. (Ford/author's collection)

Workhorses of the world

British lorries have always found ready markets abroad, thus names like Albion, Atkinson, Commer, Crossley, Dennis, ERF, Foden, Karrier, Leyland, Scammell and Thornycroft, amongst others, were familiar sights around the world.

It was not only the British Commonwealth countries to which British lorries were exported; they were to be found on every continent, and were particularly favoured in South America, a market in which Bedford was particularly successful, shipping 500 vehicles to Brazil in 1956.

The call to export during the aftermath of the Second World War meant that vehicle makers, such as Austin and Morris Commercial, sent their chassis and complete lorries to many European countries. Thornycroft specialised in supplying heavy lorries to South African Railways, Leyland made inroads to the Canadian market, while firms such as Crossley and Guy were well received on the Indian subcontinent.

The construction and petroleum industries were reliant on British technology, and it was not uncommon to see Thornycroft Big Bens and Mighty Antars working alongside Scammells and Leylands. Dumper trucks were kept busy on road-building programmes, while tractor units, including some of the largest in the world, took charge of 60-ton loads of oil pipes destined for the 560-mile-long pipeline from Kirkuk in Iran to the Mediterranean port of Baniyas.

It was also for military purposes that British lorries served abroad, from Europe to Asia and beyond, undertaking myriad duties from general supplies to transporting the heaviest tanks.

COMMER 7-TON DUMP TRUCK

Rootes exported its commercial vehicles around the world and set up sales and service arrangements in 132 countries. This 1950s advertisement shows the range of Commers and Karriers that were available, including refuse collectors, street sweepers, gully emptiers and fire engines, as well as dump trucks, tractor trailers and general purpose pick-ups.
(Author's collection)

The oilfields market was satisfied by Scammell, Thornycroft and Atkinson, the first of which is depicted here, in use as a bed truck. The Constructor was the biggest and most powerful vehicle in the Scammell catalogue, and was available in six wheelbase lengths, the bed truck having a payload of 30 tons. (Author's collection)

Scammell's 6x6 Constructor could be specified with a choice of six diesel engines, Leyland 161/200bhp, Cummins 173/212bhp, or Rolls-Royce 185/200bhp. In each case, vehicles were fitted with twelve forward and two reverse ratio gearboxes, a high degree of articulation on all wheels, and four or six-wheel drive. Shown is a self-loading flat bed truck in an oilfield environment. (Author's collection)

The petroleum and construction industries are where Thornycroft excelled, its vehicles were used to transport 60-ton loads of pipes for the installation of the 560-mile-long pipeline from Kirkuk in Iraq to the Mediterranean port of Baniyas. Though an artist's impression, this publicity item captures the Thornycroft working in hostile conditions, with dust storms a frequent hazard. (Author's collection)

The Mighty Antar, seen operating in South Africa, was claimed as Britain's largest tractor unit. The bonneted six-wheeler is nearly 32ft long and 11ft 6in wide and has two radiators mounted side-by-side, each connected to one bank of the Rover Meteorite V8 18-litre diesel engine that was developed from the Rolls-Royce Merlin V12 aero engine. The Antar (note the Thornycroft 'T' as part of the emblem) was developed as early as 1949, with deliveries commencing in 1950. (Author's collection)

This Bedford O-type lorry was photographed enduring rough conditions in Tanganyika in 1954. The terrain is demanding, but Bedfords were tough! (Bedford/author's collection)

Two mid-fifties D-type Bedford tipper trucks pictured in Rhodesia whilst working on the construction of the Kariba Dam. As is the case with the previous photograph, the road is non-existent, but that does not prevent the vehicles overcoming the harsh conditions. (Bedford/author's collection)

It might not appear huge from this picture, but ERF's heavy-duty 66R six-wheeled Tractor unit was designed to compete with Scammell and Thornycroft. Powered by Rolls-Royce's C6NFR 6-cylinder 12.2-litre diesel engine with twin cylinder heads, the tractor is fully articulated so that it can cover the most challenging terrain. Designed to work abroad, much of the production was destined for South Africa. *The Commercial Motor* cut-away drawing illustrates the rigid assembly of the chassis, along with the engine and 5-speed gearbox layout. (*Commercial Motor*/author's collection)

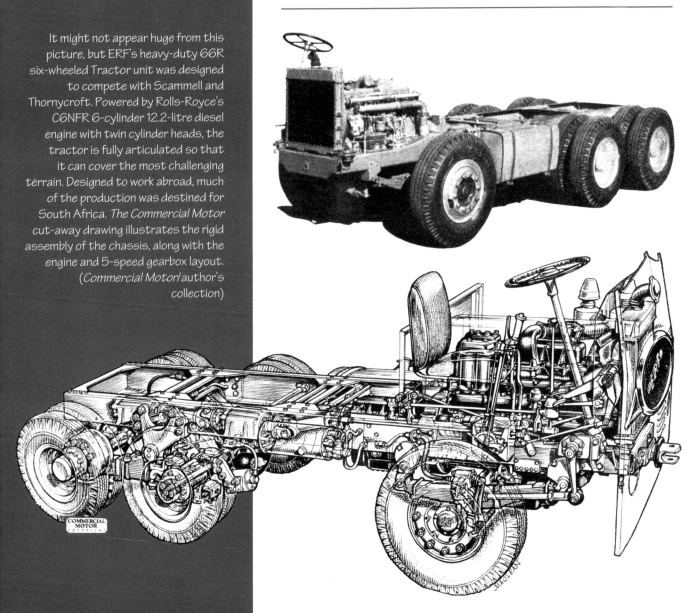

Scammell lorries were often specified for the carriage of oil and petroleum, the vehicle illustrated being one of a fleet of articulated eight-wheeler frameless spirit tankers of 4330 US gallons operated by Cia. Petrolera Shell-Mex de Cuba SA. (Author's collection)

12,000 Litres

World buyers are selective.
They need only choose the best ;
so they need only choose Tankers by . . .

THE STEEL BARREL CO LTD
UXBRIDGE · MIDDLESEX · ENGLAND

4,000 Gallons

. . . and they've got it !

*Foden F.D.6, 2 stroke Oil Engine, 126 B.H P.,
or Gardner 6 L.W. Oil Engine, 112 B.H.P.,
can be fitted as required.*

**FODENS LIMITED
SANDBACH · CHESHIRE**

(Opposite) B&B Furniture Removers Ltd of South Africa ran a 1950s FG Foden, amassing 158,000 miles in 20 months, the vehicle subjected to long distance haulage over some of the worst roads imaginable in the Union of South Africa and the Rhodesias. Foden used this Commercial Motor advertisement of April 1954 to claim the world record for the greatest trouble-free mileage. (Author's collection)

Rutland was a short-lived (1952-1956) name for a series of vehicles built by Motor Traction Ltd of New Addington in Surrey. Illustrated is the twin-steer Stuka chassis which was developed for export, and in particular fast schedules for mainland Europe operators. With its Perkins 6-cylinder R6 diesel engine and David Brown 557 gearbox, it was possible to change into top-overdrive gear at 50mph to reach a maximum of 65mph on the flat. The LHD Stuka is shown on test in Surrey and Kent. (Author's collection/*Commercial Motor*)

Bedfords made their mark around the world, the middleweight A models shown in this series of artwork illustrating the vehicles in use in foreign climes. Sales of all Bedford types in 1954, when this artwork appeared, reached 58,292 units, thus, a new factory was necessary in which to build the ever-growing range of commercials. The new works at Dunstable in Bedfordshire was ready for production in August 1955. The A model is characterised by an all-steel integral cab with its two-piece windscreen, horizontal three-slat grille and sidelamps incorporating a decorative wing flash. Though the publicity material suggests RHD vehicles, the market destinations are unclear. Whilst the Middle East market is clearly promoted, the artist chose a careful route with the pick-up and tipper models; there is an element of Canada, which could easily be interpreted as South Africa or Australia.
(Author's collection/*Commercial Motor*)

Ford supplied its Thames 2-ton Heavy-Duty Pick-up for export only, and therefore it was not a model usually seen in the United Kingdom. Built on the Thames 3.25m wheelbase chassis, the specially-designed cab seated three people, the roof extending rearwards to provide bench seat accommodation for a further three people behind the partition. (Ford publicity item/author's collection)

Heavy haulage

Few sights on the road command as much interest and depict such muscle as the movement of extraordinary loads. Railway locomotives, high-voltage generators and marine turbines, as well as industrial structures, are just a few of the items that require specialist road transport courtesy of a handful of highly experienced operators. Names such as Pickfords and Wynns come to mind, often employing Scammell, Antar and Thornycroft vehicles as well as the likes of Atkinson, ERF and Foden.

Vehicles that are engaged for heavy haulage work are giants compared to other lorries. Having enormous power, they are subjected to arduous conditions, not least much of their work being conducted crawling at a snail's pace. Drivers and crew require special training, and before any journey is undertaken careful route planning is necessary, a task that can take weeks or months to complete, taking into account obstructions such as bends, bridges, height and weight restrictions as well as road width. Safety requirements have to be addressed, such as liaising with police authorities, so that at the time of transportation the convoy has as clear passage as possible without unduly inconveniencing other road users.

In the 1950s, Britain's heavy haulage operators did not have the advantage of motorways. Industrial areas, town and city centre narrow streets as well as winding country roads had to be negotiated, which meant that specially designed tractor units and trailers had to be manoeuvred with great skill on the part of drivers and operatives.

Sheer power is portrayed in this view of a Scammell tractor unit pictured in Brighton in Sussex. Registered in 1956, this six-wheeler, named the Crimson Lady, is operated by heavy haulage contractor MC Perrett & Son. (John Curwen collection)

Gavin Wilkie Ltd was a Glasgow-based haulage contractor, and two of the firm's vehicles are seen in this image, pictured in a lay-by. The leading lorry is loaded with tyres and metal apparatus, but the load hauled by the Scammell behind is out of view. (John Curwen collection/Hub Publishing)

Askew Saw Mills' AEC with a consignment of timber, passing the Archway tavern in north London. Behind it is a Foden. Negotiating London traffic, even by early 1950s standards, would have been a difficult business. (John Curwen collection/Hub Publishing)

The size of this Scammell heavy recovery vehicle is all too obvious in this photograph taken on a wet and wintry day. Scammells were constructed for all purposes, this example appearing to have originally been used for military work.
(John Curwen collection/Truc-Foto)

SCAMMELL's...

Built to take it!

THE 4 x 4 DUMP TRUCK

The Scammell "Mountaineer" four-wheel drive Dump Truck has been exclusively designed to meet arduous demands of some "off the highway" operations. Sound engineering practice, coupled with the finest materials available, is embodied in a vehicle that will give long life and reliable and economical service during the toughest assignments.

Whether the job is local collection and delivery, long distance freight haulage, bulk liquid loads, machinery transporting, oil-fields work, etc., prospecting or pioneer work over virgin country impossible for the orthodox vehicle, there is a Scammell specially built to do it. The Scammell range of vehicles are not mass produced, but individually built by skilled craftsmen to do your specific job of work efficiently and economically.

THE 6 x 6 CONSTRUCTOR

The "Constructor" go anywhere vehicle has been ruggedly constructed to stand up to the most arduous assignment. Powered by Rolls-Royce Oil Engine, this vehicle has been designed for loads of 30—100 tons giving maximum highway or cross country performance.

SCAMMELL LORRIES LTD · WATFORD · HERTS
Telephone : WATFORD, 5231 · Telegrams : TWELFTON, WATFORD

Whether building roads or working overseas, Scammells, such as this Mountaineer four-wheel drive dump truck, were built to operate in the most arduous conditions, as this April 1954 advertisement suggests.
(Author's collection)

Pickfords was foremost in the heavy haulage industry. Seen here are two 185hp Scammell Constructor diesel tractors working front and rear of a 200-ton capacity hydraulic suspension crane trailer, transporting a GEC transformer. A policeman riding a bicycle is seen behind the rear tractor.
(Author's collection)

(Opposite) Thornycroft was another player in the heavy haulage stakes; this 1951 Nubian is pictured participating in a commercial vehicle run. Built to recover heavy lorries, this vehicle spent most of its working life operating on the A6 around Shap and the A66 trans-Pennine trunk road.
(Author's collection)

There's a lot of muscle in this evocative 1957 ERF publicity item. ERF's range of vehicles, represented here by the KV with its two-piece windscreen, wrap-around cab and oval radiator grille, extended from 6 to 50-tons capacity to include 4, 6 and 8-wheeler tippers, tankers and articulated trailers. (Author's collection)

Where strength and endurance are <u>demanded</u> . . .

ERF *is the answer*

It is the unexcelled combination of up-to-the-minute design allied with craftsman construction which enables every E.R.F. vehicle to meet the toughest conditions. They thrive on hard work, however rugged the going. Whether it's city street, country road or broken land, E.R.F. transport carries the load faster, more reliably and at lower operating cost.

In the E.R.F. range there's a model to meet every heavy transport need—from 6 to 50 tons capacity. 4-, 6- or 8-wheeler—tippers, vans, tankers and articulated trailers. Write today for full details of E.R.F. vehicles and see just how much they can help to solve your transport problems. Or ask for name of your nearest E.R.F. Dealer.

LTD. · SUN WORKS · SANDBACH · CHESHIRE

Directors: D. FODEN   E. P. FODEN   E. SHERRATT

Telephone : Sandbach 223 (5 lines)   Telegrams : E R F Sandbach

The World's Best Oil Engined Lorries

This Gardner-engined ERF, which dates from the same era as the vehicle in the previous image, was seen in 2008. Lorries like this are often to be found in the ownership of enthusiast hauliers. (Author's collection)

Heavy haulage

Scammells have always been popular with showmen and the fairground fraternity. The 45,000lb Showtrac tractor unit was designed for hauling caravans and powering fairground rides, its equipment including a 22,000lb dead pull winch and 35kW generator. The vehicle seen here was pictured when in use with Wigfield's of Stratford-upon-Avon.
(John Curwen collection/Hub Publishing)

Antar is a name associated with the oil industry, the first vehicles having been developed by Thornycroft in the late 1940s for the construction of the 560-mile-long oil pipeline between Kirkuk and the Mediterranean port of Baniyas. Since then, Antar vehicles have been seen wherever there's a need to transport extraordinary loads.
(John Curwen collection)

The Steel Barrel Co Ltd, whose premises were located on the Uxbridge Trading Estate, was a specialist builder of fuel tankers. The AEC pictured here was photographed for publicity purposes, the tanker featuring National Benzole. It is likely that the photograph was taken in the residential area adjacent to the trading estate off Cowley Mill Road. (Author's collection)

The cargo carried on this Leyland Beaver with trailer attached surely constitutes a heavy load! Driving such a vehicle as this operated by Barton's Cooperage of London E3 could not have been an easy experience, especially when negotiating narrow streets. (John Curwen collection/Truc-Foto)

Another Leyland Beaver, this time a 1953-registered 125hp vehicle pictured in London delivering Charringtons fuel oil. A feature of the Beaver cab is its attractive decorative trim detail above the air intake on each side and over the Leyland script, as well as that attached to the headlights. (John Curwen collection/Hub Publishing)

Austin's huge K9 could often be seen working alongside Bedfords and Commers pulling gun carriages and other equipment for the armed services. The vehicle pictured had been used as a mobile field office and is fitted with an awning as well as radio equipment. (Author's collection)

Pictured in the early 1950s, this Leyland Beaver tractor unit, with its 990ft^3 Bonallack aluminium-alloy bulk grain carrier, is being used for demonstration purposes. Operated by Worcestershire Farmers Ltd, the grain carrier is seen outside the firm's head office. (Author's collection)

Heavy haulage

Scammell is synonymous with Pickfords, one of the foremost names in the heavy specialist haulage industry. The lorry builder's expertise in transporting abnormal loads was acquired during the 1939-45 war, constructing all-terrain heavy vehicles, tank transporters and artillery tractors. Scammell was bought by Leyland in 1955, but it was 1960 before the firm was seen to take a new direction in the form of models it produced. (Author's collection)

This United Dairies Scammell tractor, with its specially designed trailer, is being used for publicity purposes. Scammell's articulated 6-wheelers were capable of carrying a payload of 25,000lb, dependent on tyre specification, body type and surface conditions.
(John Curwen collection/Truc-Foto)

Wearing military colours, this 1952 Scammell Explorer recovery vehicle is capable of rescuing the heaviest of lorries. Leviathans like this can always be relied upon to create interest at heritage events, such as this staged at Flookburgh on the Lancashire/Cumberland borders in 2008.
(Author's collection)

Rival to Scammell, this Mighty Antar is pictured on test between Gloucester and Ross-on-Wye in the mid-1950s. The road train, of nightmarish proportions, comprises tractors front and rear of the trailer, and is causing a tailback of traffic unable to pass on the winding road. (Author's collection)

Thornycroft's prowess in the postwar heavy haulage scene was due largely to experience gained during the war years. The huge 4x4 Nubian illustrated here was in development when hostilities began, and was extensively supplied during the war and well into the 1950s. (Author's collection)

Thornycroft, like Scammell, was absorbed into the burgeoning Leyland Empire, but not before Big Ben made its appearance. What better name to conjure up an image of power? In 1952 the model was given an 11.3-litre diesel engine, which made it ideal for general and military use. (Author's collection)

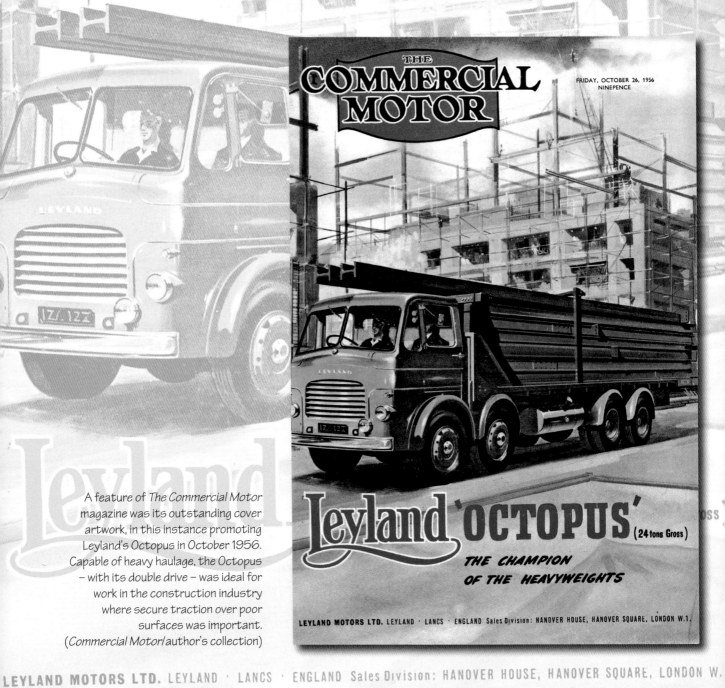

A feature of *The Commercial Motor* magazine was its outstanding cover artwork, in this instance promoting Leyland's Octopus in October 1956. Capable of heavy haulage, the Octopus – with its double drive – was ideal for work in the construction industry where secure traction over poor surfaces was important. (*Commercial Motor*/author's collection)

THE COMMERCIAL MOTOR

FRIDAY, OCTOBER 26, 1956
NINEPENCE

Leyland 'OCTOPUS' (24 tons Gross)

THE CHAMPION OF THE HEAVYWEIGHTS

LEYLAND MOTORS LTD. LEYLAND · LANCS · ENGLAND Sales Division: HANOVER HOUSE, HANOVER SQUARE, LONDON W.1.

BRITAIN'S BIGGEST TRACTOR

THORNYCROFT 'MIGHTY ANTAR'

For Gross Laden Weights

Solo 106,000 lbs. (48,000 Kgs.)
with trailer up to 224,000 lbs. (101,600 Kgs.)

'Britain's Biggest Tractor' is shown to good effect in this late 1950s publicity document. Power for the gargantuan Antar R6 tractor is supplied by a Rolls-Royce C6TFL 12-litre, 6-cylinder turbocharged diesel engine commanding 300bhp@ 2100rpm, and a top speed of 32.5mph when in auxiliary overdrive. Transmission is via a Self Changing Gear Co compounded epicyclic gearbox with air pressure operation, and comprises eight forward speeds and two reverse. (Author's collection)

The proportions of Antar's Sandmaster are evident in this brochure illustration dating from around 1957: the Morris Minor alongside the tractor unit is completely dwarfed. Technical specifications of the Sandmaster include 21.00x25 tyres, a 900 US gallon capacity fuel tank, 18ft wheelbase, Marles cam and double roller type steering with hydraulic assistance, and air pressure operated cam brakes to all wheels. (Author's collection)

Behind the scenes

The number of lorries seen on British roads during the 1950s resembled the iceberg syndrome: there was much more going on beneath the surface than was evident. When not hauling loads, vehicles needed to be cleaned, loaded, fuelled and serviced. Although the behind-the-scenes work was hardly glamorous, or as engaging as the notion of lorries in action, it was, nevertheless, of the utmost necessity. Not only did vehicle workshops undertake routine maintenance and repairs, there were breakdowns and accidents to address.

The effort of the drivers has to be remembered. Many stories abound of those behind the wheel with great determination to get to their destination on time, in an era before the dreaded tachograph. Then there are the prosaic duties of municipal vehicles to consider; collecting refuse, clearing drains, maintaining highways, among others. Essential, too, were the seemingly humdrum mobile shops that took supplies to out-of-town housing estates and remote rural areas – the tasks they performed were as much social-minded as they were commercial, being beneficial to shoppers for whom car ownership was but a dream.

Taking the behind-the-scenes activities a stage further, development and testing of new models should not be forgotten. Before a type of lorry could enter service, it had to satisfy a huge criteria of tests aimed at maintaining safety for drivers, operators, pedestrians and other road users.

The premises of Arlington Motor Co Ltd of Ipswich as seen in the mid-1950s when the company was agent for Bedford, Leyland and Dennis. Behind the railings is a variety of vehicles for sale, including a Bedford OB bus and pick-up. The extent of the premises can be judged by the size of the workshop behind the showroom frontage.
(Richard Burn/author's collection)

The interior of cider-maker HP Bulmer's workshops is shown in this October 1956 advertisement sponsoring Laycock lifts. Furthest from the camera is a Hillman car or Commer van; next to it a Foden, and, in the foreground, an ERF and Leyland Comet. Not all commercial vehicle workshops were as clean and tidy as this!
(*Commercial Motor*/author's collection)

Behind the scenes work included coachbuilding. This photograph shows a variety of lorry bodies being constructed, mainly, it would appear, for Bedford chassis. In some instances wooden framework has been constructed, onto which aluminium sheeting has been fitted. (D Cook/author's collection)

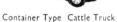

Plastics bodywork, exemplified here by Samlesbury Engineering, was a feature found on some lorries. The coachbuilding process, using Bakelite polyester resin and glass fibre, allowed for excellent weight to strength ratio, and a well-lit interior. (Author's collection)

Foremost a commercial coachbuilder, JH Jennings & Son of Sandbach, Cheshire (home to ERF and Foden) built bodies for all types of chassis, and was particularly noted for furniture vans, horseboxes, cattle trucks, and mobile shops. (Author's collection)

A lorry's unclothed chassis is normally not seen. Illustrated is a 1950 Seddon Mark 7 with a Perkins P4 1924cc 4-cylinder diesel engine. Three chassis types were available: the 7L with a 10ft 6in wheelbase for goods work, the 7S8 with an 8ft 6in wheelbase for tipper work, and 7S6 with a 6ft 10in wheelbase built as a tractor unit. (Author's collection)

Adaptable . . .

to all types of bodywork

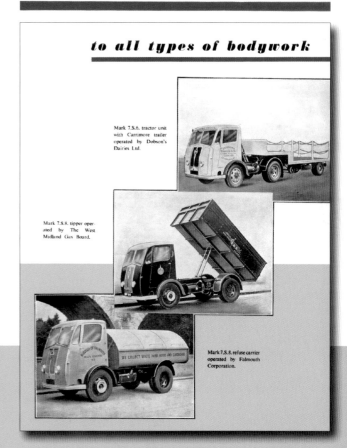

Mark 7.S.6. tractor unit with Carrimore trailer operated by Dobson's Dairies Ltd.

Mark 7.S.8. tipper operated by The West Midland Gas Board.

Mark 7.S.8. refuse carrier operated by Falmouth Corporation.

Seddons were specified by independent hauliers as well as the utilities and local authorities. Here, the Seddon catalogue shows the Mark 7 in use with Falmouth Corporation, the West Midland Gas Board, and Dobson's Dairies of Levenshulme. (Author's collection)

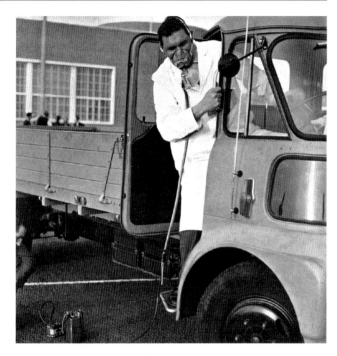

(Above) Another test conducted by Professor Drew was to assess driver fatigue. A vehicle has been fitted with special measuring equipment in place of the passenger cushion to record the amount of grip exerted by the driver. (Author's collection)

Testing lorries was a necessary operation, in this instance being carried out in 1959 on the then-new Austin Series 4 5-ton truck. Tests were carried out by Professor G Drew M.A., Professor of Psychology at the University of London, where the amount of energy and oxygen a driver uses in getting in and out of a cab is being established. (Author's collection)

Shelvoke and Drewry vehicles were popular with local authorities; this 1948-registered example is pictured in Southend-on-Sea in the mid-1950s. SD specialised in refuse collectors, and in this instance the vehicle has a waste paper trailer. SDs were designed for working in restricted areas. (Author's collection)

(Above and opposite) Karrier was another favourite with municipal undertakings, the Bantam and Gamecock models being available in a variety of body styles. Shown on this lovely publicity item are the Bantam 2266cc petrol-engined, all-steel dust cart, and 2-ton Highways tipper, both of which were designed with a 32ft turning circle.

(Rootes Group publicity item/author's collection)

'The Perfect Shop On Wheels' was the message when promoting the Karrier Bantam range of mobile shops. The design of the vehicle allowed customers to step aboard rather than have to queue outside; likewise, the driver and assistant had walk-through access from the cab to the sales area. This emotive publicity item depicts happy shoppers on a surreal housing estate where the sun is always shining. (Rootes Group publicity item/author's collection)

For long service on short-haul work

★ *World-famous Battery manufacturers are among the many users of the Scammell system.*

Throughout the world, operators in all fields of transport in ever increasing numbers are proving beyond doubt that the Scarab Mechanical Horse, with its extreme manœuvrability, versatility, and interchangeability of trailers, provides the most economical and efficient distributive service unequalled by any other form of transport. The Scammell system will provide the most economical answer to your short-haul problems.

★ Interchangeability ensures greater carrying power.

The SCAMMELL
scarab
MECHANICAL HORSE

Further details of the Scammell system gladly sent on request.

SCAMMELL LORRIES LIMITED · WATFORD · HERTS.   Phone: Watford 5231

Jensen Motors Ltd is not a name usually associated with commercial vehicles. Nevertheless, this constructor of prestigious cars made available a range of commercial and military models, including the Ford 1172cc side-valve, petrol-engined Jen-Tug, which had its design origins immediately prewar. This 1953 publicity image shows the Jen-Tug in service with Portsmouth coal merchant F Sprake.
(Author's collection)

Nipping around factory areas out of the public gaze is what the Scammell Scarab did well. This October 1956 advertisement shows a Mechanical Horse in the employment of battery manufacturer Eveready.
(Author's collection)

An essential behind-the-scenes aspect of lorry manufacturing is component manufacturing. Automotive Products Company Limited was a major supplier to the road haulage industry and, as this publicity item shows, produced Thompson ball joints and tie rods. An ERF tanker unit, Guy tipper, and an Atkinson flatbed lorry are featured. (Author's collection)

They all fit Steering Safety

Thompson

BALL JOINTS & TIE RODS
The safest mode

STAND **359** COMMERCIAL MOTOR SHOW EARLS COURT Sept. 21-29

AUTOMOTIVE PRODUCTS COMPANY LIMITED · LEAMINGTON SPA · WARWICKSHIRE

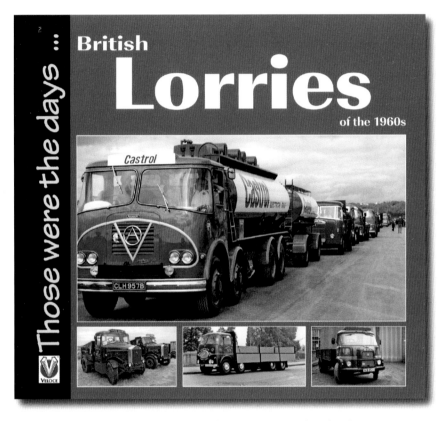

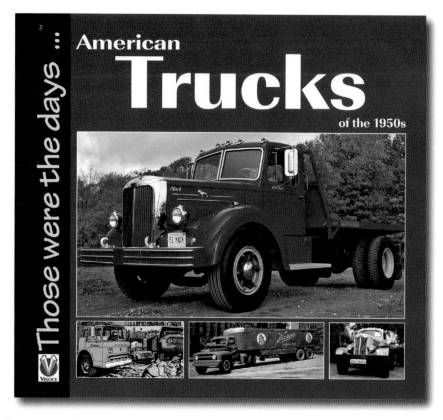

This highly visual study examines the important role of trucks and trucking in the 1950s, recounting the essential role it played in the industrial growth of the US and Canada. Features factory photos, advertisements, original truck brochures and restored examples, plus a comprehensive guide to all models produced.

£14.99
ISBN: 978-1-84584-227-7

For more info on Veloce titles, visit our website at www.veloce.co.uk
email info@veloce.co.uk • tel: +44 (0)1305 260068 • prices subject to change • p+p extra

More *Those were the days ...* titles from Veloce Publishing –

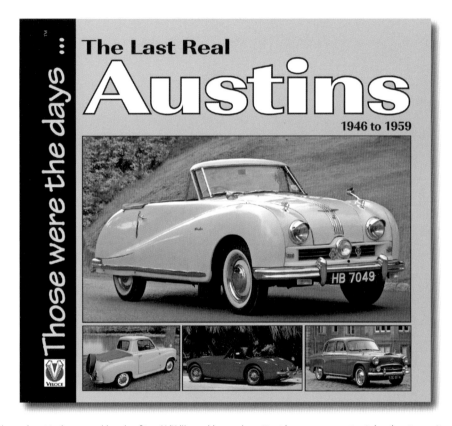

This book examines how Austin bounced back after WWII, and how, despite the severe materials shortage, it managed to develop the largest range of vehicles produced by any automaker in postwar Britain. Illustrated with 100 pictures, many of them archive photographs, depicting the weird, and wonderful – and the downright imaginative.

£14.99
ISBN: 978-1-84584-193-5

For more info on Veloce titles, visit our website at www.veloce.co.uk
email info@veloce.co.uk • tel: +44 (0)1305 260068 • prices subject to change • p+p extra

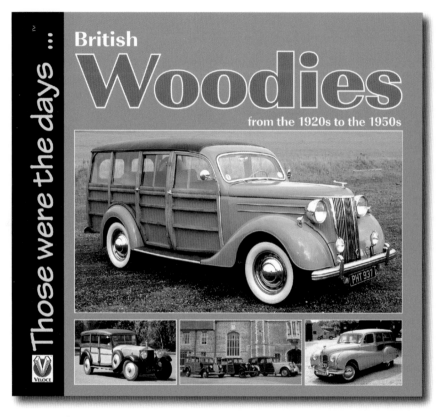

Highlighting the work of hundreds of small coachbuilders, and illustrated with 100 rare and previously unpublished photographs, this book is a tribute to the skills of the people who built these amazing wooden wonders.

£12.99
ISBN: 978-1-84584-169-0

For more info on Veloce titles, visit our website at www.veloce.co.uk
email info@veloce.co.uk • tel: +44 (0)1305 260068 • prices subject to change • p+p extra

Index